CRIME SCENE INVESTIGATION

THE CRIME SCENE PUZZLE

BY DONNA McKINNEY

BLASTOFF! DISCOVERY

BLASTOFF! DISCOVERY, AN IMPRINT OF BELLWETHER MEDIA BY FLUTTERBEE

This edition first published in 2027 by Bellwether Media, Inc.

Bellwether Media is a division of FlutterBee Education Group.

For information regarding permission, write to Bellwether Media, Inc., Attention: Permissions Department,
3500 American Blvd W, Suite 150, Bloomington, MN 55431.

Library of Congress Cataloging-in-Publication Data is available at www.loc.gov or upon request from the publisher.

ISBN: 9798898800840 (hardcover)
ISBN: 9798898802080 (ebook)

Editor: Rachael Barnes Series Designer: Josh Brink

Printed in the United States of America, North Mankato, MN.

TABLE OF CONTENTS

WHAT IS THE CRIME SCENE PUZZLE

CRIME SCENE INVESTIGATORS

Imagine a table full of scattered jigsaw puzzle pieces. Solvers look for common colors and shapes to connect the pieces. The puzzle picture starts to become clear. When a crime takes place, important clues are often left behind. These pieces of **evidence** are the puzzle pieces of the crime.

Crime scene investigators (CSIs) are puzzle solvers. Their job involves finding evidence. Every piece is important. They connect the pieces to create a picture of the crime. Putting the pieces together correctly can make or break a case. The work begins at the scene of the crime.

COLLECTING EVIDENCE

For hundreds of years, police had limited clues to solve crimes. They talked to witnesses. They looked for visible evidence. In 1910, Edmond Locard opened a **forensic laboratory**, or lab, in France. Locard believed it was impossible for criminals to be at a crime scene without leaving evidence behind. Locard's idea was correct! Using science to solve crimes became the field of forensic science.

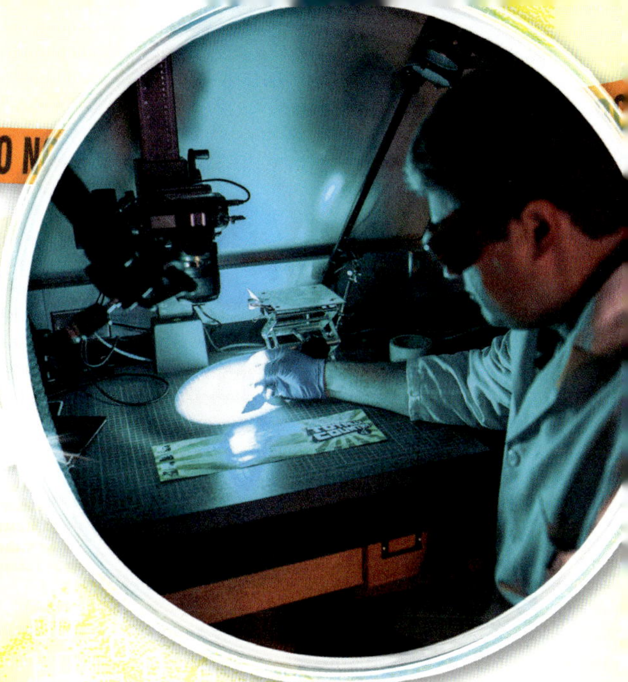

Today, CSIs use the latest technology to collect evidence. Then the evidence is studied. It provides clues that help police connect **suspects** to a crime scene.

STATS

MOST COMMON NONVIOLENT CRIME: **burglary**

COMMON CSI EDUCATION: **2 to 6 years** of college

CSI AVERAGE ANNUAL PAY: **$59,636** a year

AT THE CRIME SCENE

CSIs arrive at the crime scene. It could be on a road or sidewalk or in a house. CSIs use brightly colored tape to block off the spaces where evidence is located. This keeps evidence safe until CSIs can collect it. They look for fingerprints. Some are visible. Others known as latent prints are difficult to see. They are left by sweat and oil from the skin.

NOT CROSS

CRIME SCENE DO NOT

CSIs use powerful lights to find latent prints. They also apply dark powders to reveal these fingerprints. This is called dusting. They carefully photograph all prints. Then they "lift" latent prints from surfaces with clear tape.

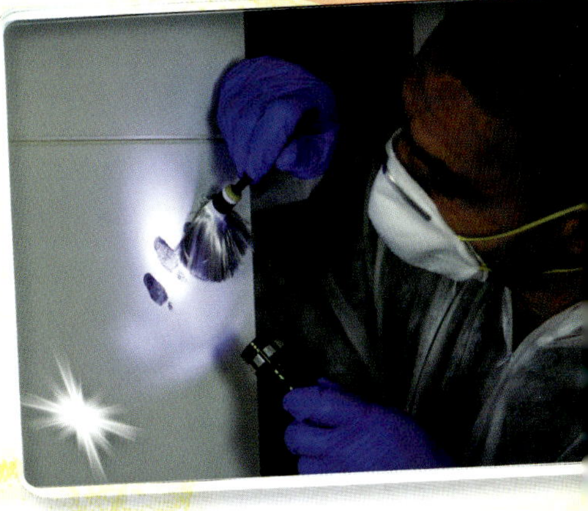

SEARCH PATTERNS

CSIs search some crime scenes in straight lines. They may divide the scene into zones. Sometimes they search in a spiral, working out from a piece of evidence.

CSIs collect **DNA** evidence. People leave their DNA in blood, flakes of skin, saliva, and more. Every person's DNA is different. DNA can show who was at the crime scene.

DNA samples can be collected by swabbing surfaces with clean cotton swabs. Scraping with clean razor blades is another common collection method. For some DNA samples, CSIs may cut out pieces of fabric or carpet.

COLLECTING A DNA SAMPLE

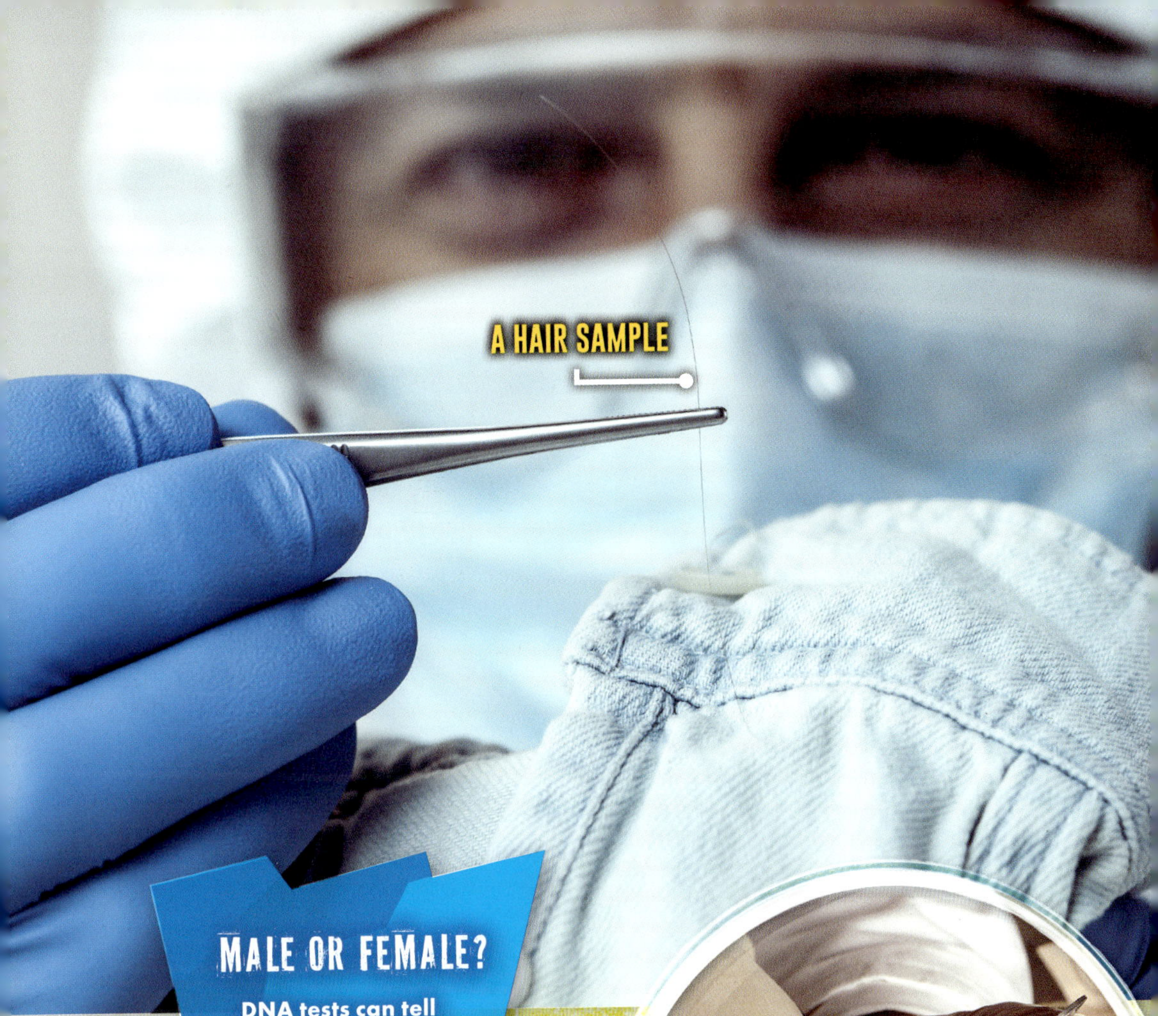

MALE OR FEMALE?

DNA tests can tell scientists whether a suspect is male or female.

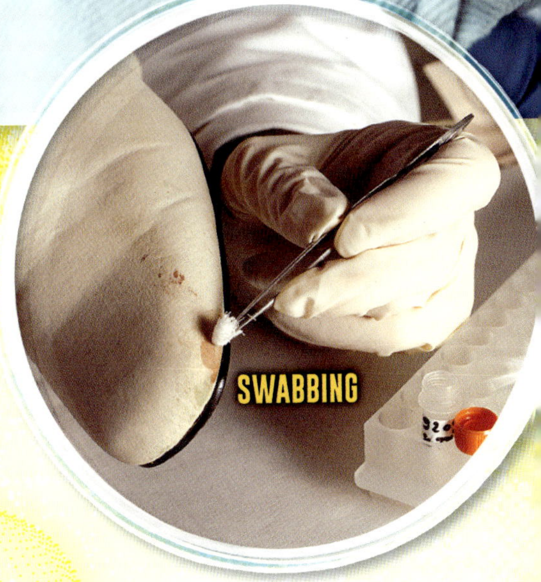

Small things like fingernails, hair, or toothpicks might hold DNA. These small pieces are **trace evidence**. CSIs place these items in envelopes. They seal and label each envelope.

THAT IS STICKY!

CSIs use special super sticky tape to gather evidence off smooth or flat surfaces. Tape can collect fingerprints, footprints, and tire tracks.

Footprints and tire tracks are useful pattern evidence. Suspects can leave footprints or tire tracks at the crime scene. Muddy footprints and tire tracks are easy to see. Plastic patterns are found in soft surfaces. This type of pattern is often pressed into sand, snow, or mud. Latent patterns are often found on wood floors or paved roads. They cannot be seen with the naked eye.

CSIs take careful photos of all visible and plastic patterns. They may use **casting** to make copies of plastic patterns. They use lasers to collect some latent footprints. The lasers create detailed images.

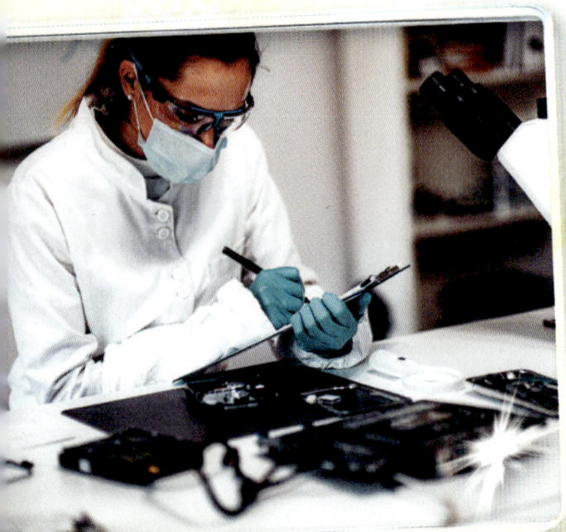

Forensic analysts are called in to investigate **cybercrimes**. Criminals use computers for a variety of cybercrimes. They steal money. They steal people's personal information. They conduct illegal businesses.

CRIME SCENE DO NOT CROSS

Analysts search for clues on computers, cell phones, and tablets. They search **hard drives** and **servers**. Analysts uncover the data on these devices. They can see a suspect's digital activity. They track communications and web searches. CSIs gather all of these pieces of evidence. Evidence helps them link a suspect to the crime. The crime scene puzzle picture becomes more clear.

HOW MUCH?

Over $16 billion was lost to cybercrimes in 2024.

CASE FILE

NINTENDO SWITCH

CRIME murder of Professor Matthew Wiser

YEAR OF THE CRIME 2019

HOW IT WAS SOLVED Professor Matthew Wiser was killed when thieves broke into his house. They stole a Nintendo Switch. Police used emails and a serial number to identify the Switch. They tracked the Switch to a home where it had been reconnected to the internet. This led them to the two men who committed the murder.

SOLVING THE CRIME SCENE PUZZLE

FORENSIC SCIENTIST WORKING WITH FINGERPRINT EVIDENCE

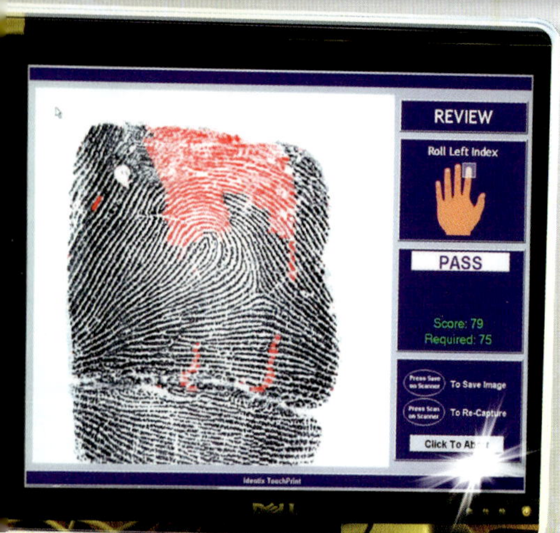

After CSIs collect crime scene evidence, it goes to the forensic lab. **Forensic scientists** study the evidence. Scientists used to study fingerprints with magnifying glasses. Today they mainly use computers. Computers scan fingerprint evidence. Scientists **analyze** the digital images. They study the patterns of ridges in the prints.

State police and the Federal Bureau of Investigation (FBI) have large **databases** of known fingerprints. The databases provide lists of potential matches. Scientists compare crime scene prints with database prints. Scientists analyze the prints to find an exact match. They record their conclusions.

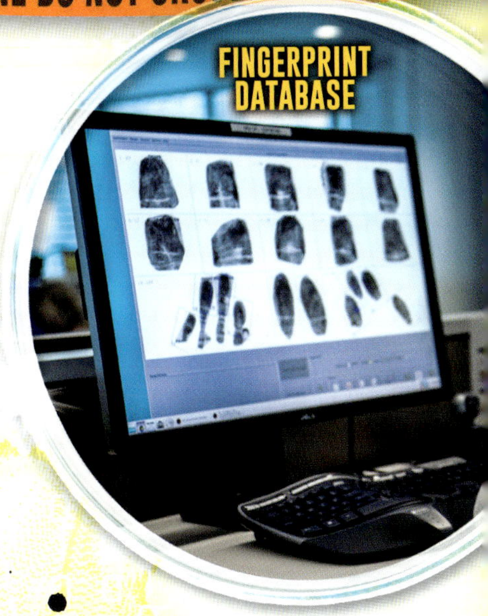

CASE FILE

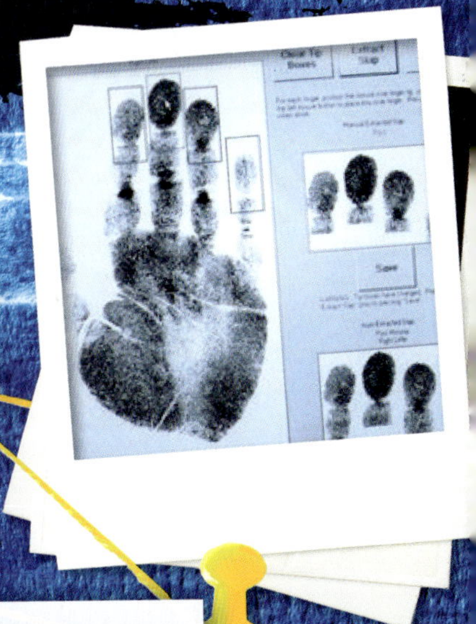

CRIME robbery and murder cold case

YEAR OF THE CRIME 1983

YEAR SOLVED 2010

HOW IT WAS SOLVED A robber broke into a hotel room where two men were watching TV. The robber shot and killed one man and badly injured the other. He stole items and escaped. Police collected 23 latent fingerprints from the crime scene. But they had no suspects for over 25 years. In 2010, police found a fingerprint match in the FBI database. The suspect was caught and sent to prison. Cold case solved!

Scientists analyze DNA samples. They use lab machines to make copies of the samples. Now scientists can run many tests. DNA samples are separated into smaller pieces. This is where unique patterns can be found in DNA.

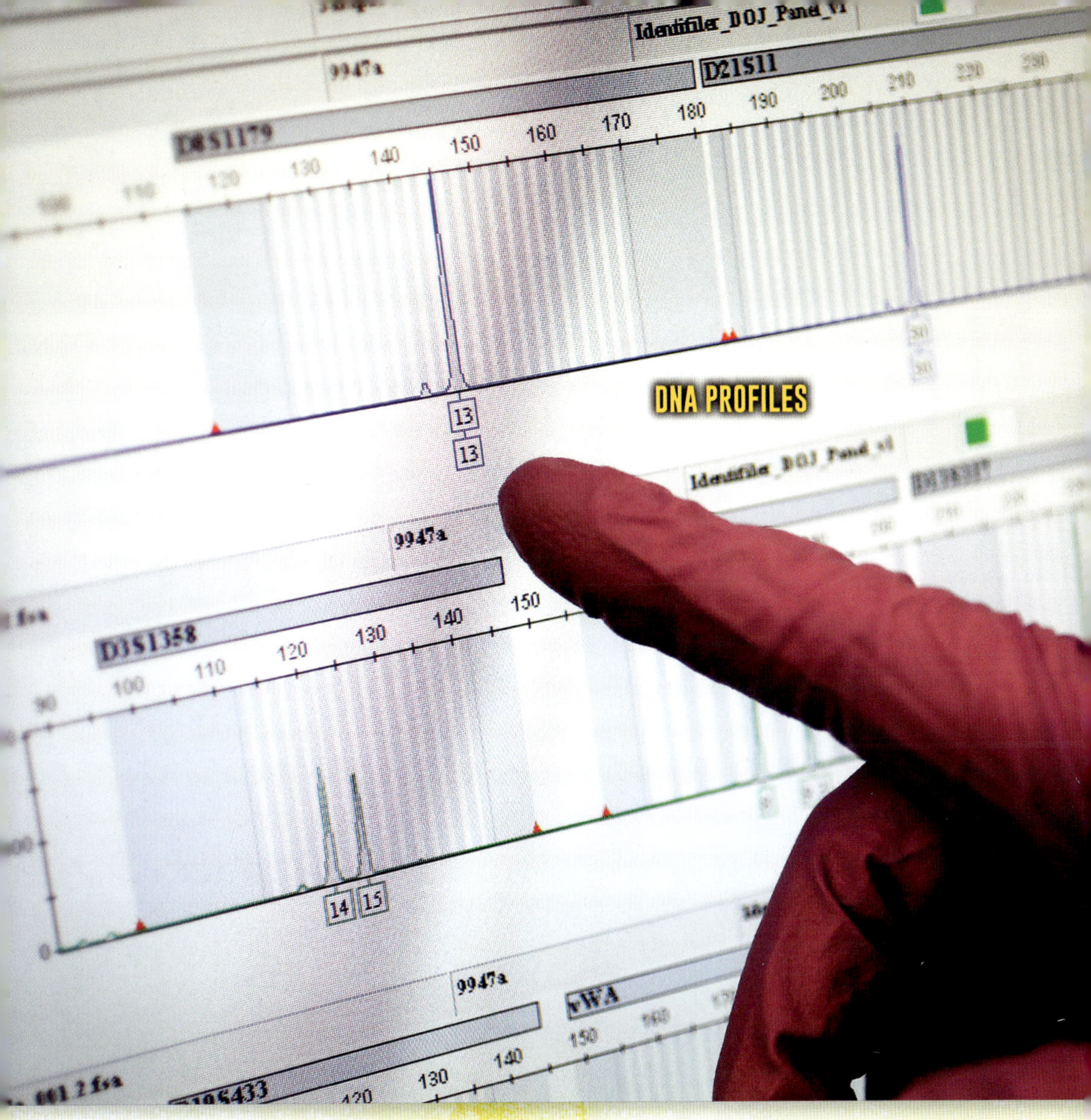

DNA PROFILES

Scientists create **DNA profiles** from the test results. They compare the DNA profiles to the national DNA database. The database provides some partial matches. It is difficult to tell different human DNA apart. There are only a few unique parts in every person's DNA. Scientists search digital results to find these unique markers. Scientists work to give clear evidence to CSIs on the case.

Footprint and tire track evidence are also sent to the lab for study. Scientists examine the patterns. They use **microscopes** and special lights. They identify the size and general tread patterns. They also look for worn places on the patterns. They note unique marks, including nicks or cuts on the footprint or tire track.

Special **software** helps scientists see the tiny details in crime scene photos. Then scientists search databases. The databases give them a list of shoes or tires that have similar patterns. Scientists decide if the patterns connect to a specific shoe or tire.

CRIME SCENE DO NOT CROSS

TESTING A POWDER SAMPLE

Many forensic tests rely on chemistry. Scientists use chemistry to study evidence brought to the lab. This evidence is often a sample of a powder, liquid, or stain. Scientists use different machines to detect tiny amounts of substances, such as drugs or poisons.

For cybercrimes, analysts search for digital patterns that are clues to crimes. They use special tools to create forensic images. These are exact copies of data on devices. They can investigate without changing the evidence. Analysts study internet use, messages, and email. They look for hidden data. They track how money is moved when it is stolen.

As all of the evidence is collected and tested, CSIs use forms to keep track of the **chain of custody**. They use the forms to record when the evidence was collected. CSIs note where evidence was stored. They list the people who worked with the evidence. These forms prove the evidence was not tampered with during the investigation.

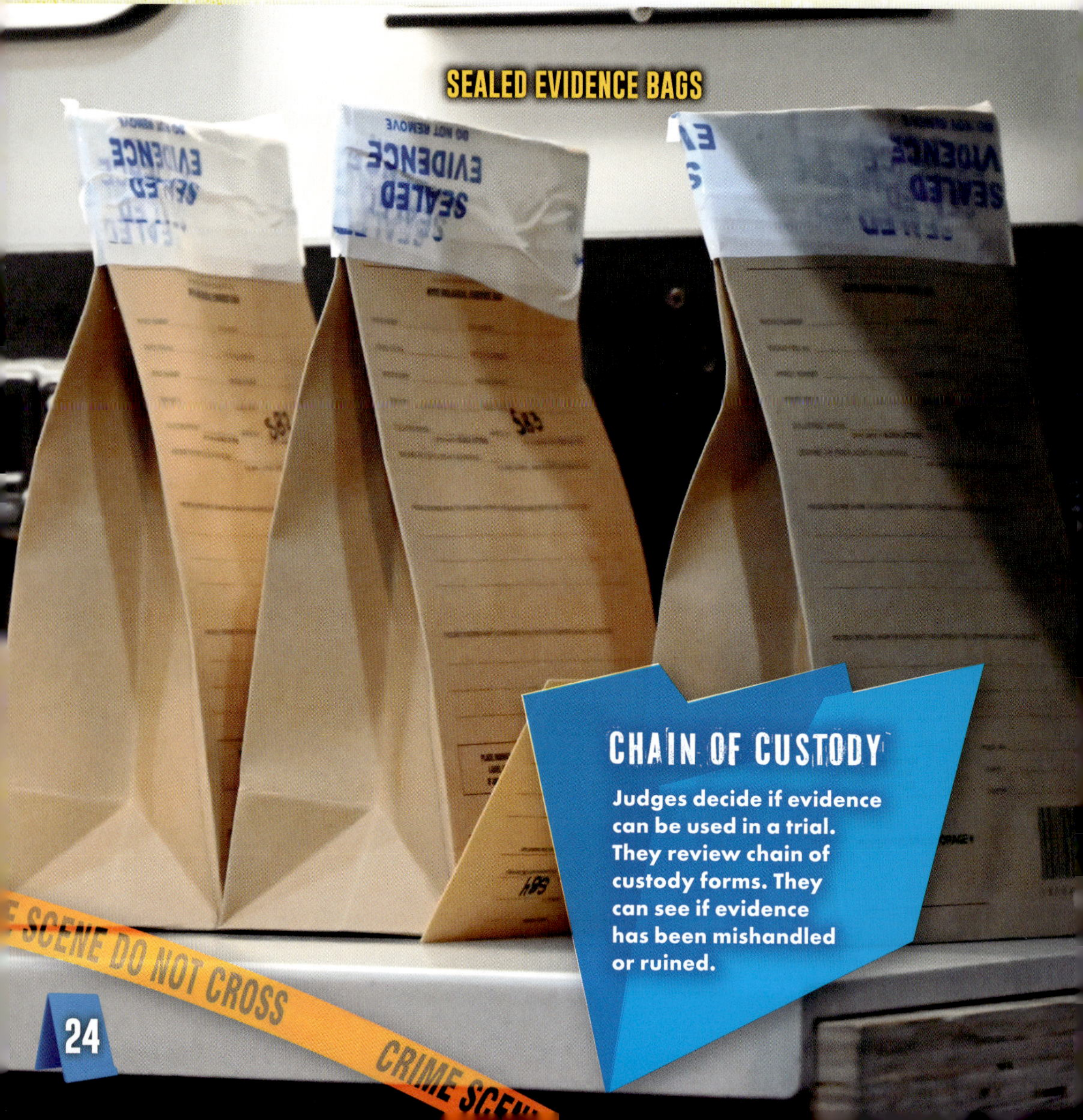

SEALED EVIDENCE BAGS

CHAIN OF CUSTODY

Judges decide if evidence can be used in a trial. They review chain of custody forms. They can see if evidence has been mishandled or ruined.

CHALLENGES

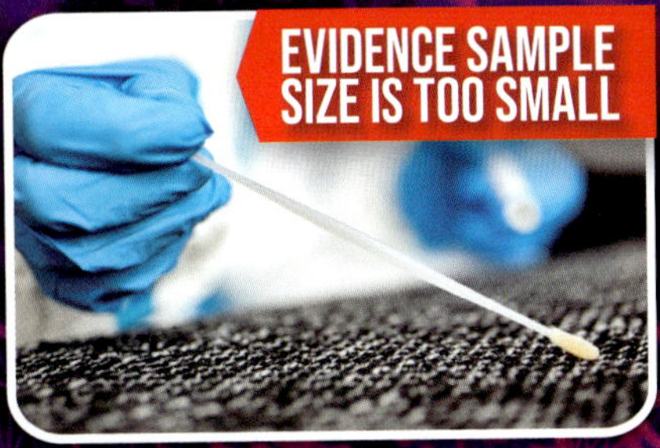

CSIs and scientists face challenges. Evidence samples may be too small for testing. Weather can damage the evidence at outdoor crime scenes. CSIs and other workers can accidentally add their DNA to crime scenes. The chain of custody might be unclear. Even with these challenges, experts work together to solve the puzzle.

THE FUTURE OF CRIME SCENE INVESTIGATION

Portable, or easily moved, tools are changing how CSIs work at crime scenes. Portable microscopes help CSIs find evidence. CSIs can begin studying bullets, hair, fibers, and fingerprints. Handheld microscopes connect to computers. This lets CSIs use digital images to analyze tiny details. Lights used to find latent prints are becoming more portable too.

Portable **spectrometers** help CSIs identify substances like drugs, explosives, and other chemicals. They help CSIs find and collect trace evidence. Analysis that used to be done in the lab can now be started at the crime scene.

GAS CHROMATOGRAPHY-MASS SPECTROMETRY (GC-MS)

YEAR INVENTED

1955

WHAT IS IT?

Gas chromatography (GC) and mass spectrometry (MS) started out as two separate laboratory tools. GC separates chemical mixtures. MS can identify the different parts of the mixture. In 1955, two scientists joined the tools together. Over the years, GC-MS has been improved. Today CSIs use portable GC-MS tools. They can quickly identify drugs, explosives, and dangerous chemicals at the crime scene. GC-MS tools are essential at the crime scene and in the forensics lab.

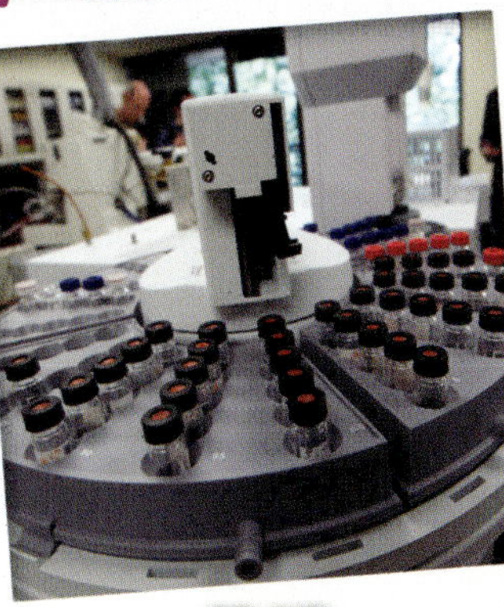

GC-MS

POLICE USING AI FOR FACIAL RECOGNITION

Artificial intelligence (AI) plays a growing role in forensic science. AI helps find and match fingerprint patterns. It can create profiles to recognize faces and DNA. It can match pattern evidence using partial footprints or tire tracks. AI helps forensic analysts study huge sets of computer data. While AI is still improving, it is already a powerful tool for CSIs and scientists.

Piece by piece, CSIs and scientists assemble the crime scene puzzle. Reports and conclusions based on evidence work to create a clear picture. CSIs often catch suspects. Scientists may share their conclusions in court cases. These final pieces lead to a decision on suspects' guilt or innocence. Case closed!

FORENSIC SCIENTIST IN COURT

GLOSSARY

analyze–to look carefully at something to understand and identify its important parts

artificial intelligence–a computer's ability to do things a human mind can do

casting–the process of pouring a substance into a space to create a 3D model of the shape

chain of custody–the written record of everyone who handles a piece of evidence from the time it is collected until it goes to court

crime scene investigators–people who collect and analyze evidence found at crime scenes

cybercrimes–crimes committed using computers and the internet

databases–digital systems used to store and sort data

DNA–related to a tiny substance that carries information about the makeup of a living thing

DNA profiles–sets of DNA patterns or types that are unique to each person

evidence–a witness statement or an item or impression found at a crime scene that links a suspect to a crime

forensic analysts–people who use scientific methods to study digital evidence

forensic laboratory–a place where scientists perform tests to study evidence left at a crime scene

forensic scientists–people who use scientific methods to study physical evidence

hard drives–parts inside computers that store data

microscopes–laboratory tools that make tiny things look much bigger

servers–computers in networks that provide services to other computers in the network

software–computer programs that do specific tasks

spectrometers–instruments that separate light into colors to see different wavelengths

suspects–people the police believe may have committed a crime

trace evidence–evidence that is too small to be easily seen

TO LEARN MORE

AT THE LIBRARY

Campbell, Grace. *Crime Scene Evidence*. Minneapolis, Minn.: Lerner Publications, 2021.

Hamilton, John. *Forensics*. Minneapolis, Minn.: Abdo & Daughters Publishing, 2022.

Ross, Melissa. *Forensics for Kids: The Science and History of Crime Solving with 21 Activities*. Chicago, Ill.: Chicago Review Press, 2022.

ON THE WEB

FACTSURFER

Factsurfer.com gives you a safe, fun way to find more information.

1. Go to www.factsurfer.com.
2. Enter "the crime scene puzzle" into the search box and click 🔍.
3. Select your book cover to see a list of related content.

INDEX

The images in this book are reproduced through the courtesy of: Ignatiev, front cover; Jeff McCollough, pp. 2 (evidence marker 1), 3 (evidence marker 3); Uri, p. 3 (evidence marker 2); Steve Sanchez Photos, pp. 4-5; PRESSLAB, p. 5 (bottom); haikeiya, p. 5 (jigsaw puzzle); Keystone/ Stringer/ Getty Images, p. 6; David Brewster/ Minneapolis Star Tribune/ Alamy Stock Photo, p. 7; Melnikov Dmitriy, p. 7 (top); FBI Media/ Federal Bureau of Investigation, pp. 7 (middle), 17 (all), 18 (top), 26, 28; bunyarit klinsukhon, p. 7 (bottom); Fuss Sergey, p. 8 (top); Joe Raedle/ Getty Images, p. 8; zoka74, p. 9 (top); MUSTAFA OZER/ AFP/ Getty Images, p. 9; Julian Stratenschulte/ picture alliance/ Getty Images, p. 10; D-Keine, p. 11 (top); Alexis ORAND/ Gamma-Rapho/ Getty Images, p. 11; Couperfield, pp. 12 (top), 13 (all); kilukilu, p. 12; Mark Boster/ Los Angeles Times/ Getty Images, p. 14 (top); Microgen, p. 14; Christian Bertrand, p. 15; David R. Frazier Photolibrary, Inc./ Alamy Stock Photo, p. 16 (top); Robert Nickelsberg/ Getty Images, p. 16; miodrag ignjatovic, p. 18; Al Seib/ Getty Images, p. 19; Grzegorz Kozakiewicz/ Alamy Stock Photo, pp. 20-21; Zoonar/ Elnur Amikishiyev/ Alamy Stock Photo, p. 21; Dave Martin/ AP Images, pp. 22-23; Steve Helber/ AP Newsroom, p. 23; Kyle Mazza/ AP Newsroom, p. 24; Robert Kneschke, p. 25 (challenges top left); Gorodenkoff, p. 25 (challenges top right); Oxygen_project, p. 25 (challenges bottom); Christoph Reichwein/ Getty Images, p. 25; Rolf Vennenbernd/ Getty Images, p. 27 (top); PAUL J. RICHARDS/ AFP/ Getty Images, p. 27; Boris Roessler/ picture alliance/ Getty Images, p. 28; Luis Sánchez Saturno-Pool/ Getty Images, p. 29.